I0103602

Anonymous

Minutes of the Organization and Proceedings

of the New England Soldiers' Relief Association. Printed for the

Association.

Anonymous

Minutes of the Organization and Proceedings
of the New England Soldiers' Relief Association. Printed for the Association.

ISBN/EAN: 9783337308063

Printed in Europe, USA, Canada, Australia, Japan

Cover: Foto ©Suzi / pixelio.de

More available books at **www.hansebooks.com**

MINUTES

ORGANIZATION AND PROCEEDINGS

OF THE

New England Soldiers' Relief Association.

194 Broadway, New York.

OFFICERS.

WILLIAM M. EVARTS, Chairman.
CHARLES GOULD, Vice-Chairman.
SAMUEL E. LOW, Treasurer.
WM. H. L. BARNES, Corresponding Secretary.
WILLIAM BOND, ⎱ Secretaries.
MAURICE PERKINS, ⎰
COL. FRANK E. HOWE, Superintendent.

Printed for the Association.

ROOT, ANTHONY & CO.

1862.

New England Soldiers' Relief Association.

194 Broadway.

———— • • ————

CHAIRMAN,	WILLIAM M. EVARTS, Esq.
VICE-CHAIRMAN,	CHARLES GOULD, Esq.
TREASURER,	SAMUEL E. LOW, Esq.
CORRESPONDING SECRETARY,	WM. H. L. BARNES, Esq.
SECRETARIES,	WILLIAM BOND, Esq.
	DR. MAURICE PERKINS.
SUPERINTENDENT,	COL. FRANK E. HOWE.

MAINE.

DEXTER A. HAWKINS, Esq., STATE AGENT, 10 Wall street.
WILLIAM H. FOGG, Esq., 32 Burling Slip.
REV. R. D. HITCHCOCK, D. D., 149 East 12th street.

NEW HAMPSHIRE.

HON. BENJ. W. BONNEY, 128 Broadway.
HON. CHARLES A. PEABODY, 60 Wall street.
JEREMIAH BURNS, Esq., Astor House.

VERMONT.

E. W. STOUGHTON, Esq., 72 Wall street.
MAJ. J. A. PULLEN, 74 Broadway.
JOHN PAINE, Esq., 47 Wall street.

MASSACHUSETTS.

COL. FRANK E. HOWE, STATE AGENT, 194 Broadway.
F. E. WELLINGTON, Esq., 63 Ann street.
SAMUEL E. LOW, Esq., 31 Burling Slip.

RHODE ISLAND.

NEHEMIAH KNIGHT, Esq., 56 Park Place.
WILLIAM J. HOPPIN, Esq., 61 Pine street.
REV. FRANCIS VINTON, D. D., Trinity Church.

CONNECTICUT.

COL. JOHN H. ALMY, STATE AGENT, 137 Broadway.
GEN. PROSPER M. WETMORE, 30 Pine street.
CHARLES GOULD, Esq., 2 Hanover street.

WILLIAM M. EVARTS, Esq., 2 Hanover street.
WILLIAM BOND, Esq., 21 Nassau street.
DR. MAURICE PERKINS, College of Physicians and Surgeons.
SAMUEL W. BRIDGHAM, 24 Waverly Place.
COL. GEORGE BLISS, JR, 50 Wall street.
DR. ELEAZAR PARMLY, 3 Bond street.

ROBERT H. McCURDY, Esq., 45 Park Place.
REV. H. W. BELLOWS, D. D., 59 East 20th street.
REV. SAMUEL OSGOOD, D. D., 154 West 11th street.
WILLIAM H. L. BARNES, Esq., 62 Wall street.
HON. RUFUS F. ANDREWS, 47 Wall street.
HOSEA B. PERKINS, Esq., 98 Bowery.

Finance Committee.

SAMUEL E. LOW, Esq., CHAIRMAN.

WILLIAM H. FOGG, Esq., Maine.
CHAS. A. PEABODY, Esq., N. H.
JOHN PAINE, Esq., Vermont.

F. E. WELLINGTON, Esq., Mass.
NEHEMIAH KNIGHT, Esq., R. I.
CHARLES GOULD, Esq., Conn.

Honorary Members.

GOVERNOR ANDREW, OF MASS.
" SPRAGUE, OF R. I.
" BUCKINGHAM, OF CT.

GOVERNOR HOLBROOK, OF VT.
" WASHBURNE, OF ME.
" BERRY, OF N. H.

GOVERNOR MORGAN, OF N. Y.

"NEW ENGLAND

"SOLDIERS' RELIEF ASSOCIATION."

PRELIMINARY MEETING AND ORGANIZATION.

In pursuance of arrangements made at a preliminary meeting of gentlemen held at the Astor House, on the 28th of March, 1862, and in accordance with a public notice given in the daily papers of the city, a large and influential meeting of citizens of New England resident in New York, was held at the Fifth Avenue Hotel, on Monday evening, March 31, 1862, with the purpose of making arrangements to provide for proper attention to the sick and wounded soldiers as they shall from time to time pass through New York on their return from the seat of war to their homes.

Mr. William M. Evarts was chosen Chairman of the meeting, and Mr. William Bond and Dr. Maurice Perkins were chosen Secretaries.

After a long discussion of the subject, which was participated in by the following gentlemen, viz., Mr. Charles Gould, Gen. Prosper M. Wetmore, Mr. George W. Blunt, Rev. Dr. F. Vinton, Col. George Bliss, Capt. E. E. Morgan, Col. Frank E. Howe, Mr. Nath. Hayden, Hon. C. A. Peabody, Dr. James R. Wood, Mr. C. C. Leigh, Mr. William M. Evarts, Dr. J. H. Griscom, and others, the following resolutions were unanimously adopted:

1. *Resolved*, That a committee be appointed by the Chair, of three from each New England State, with power to fill vacancies, and to add to their number, to provide the necessary means, and to provide suitable care, attendance, and accommodations for the sick, disabled and wounded

New England soldiers as they pass through the city on their way homeward from the war; and that the citizens, physicians, and surgeons of New York, and the United States Sanitary Commission, be invited to coöperate in this patriotic and benevolent plan.

2. *Resolved*, That this committee be instructed, that in performing their duties to the sick and wounded of New England, they extend their aid and charity to their comrades from every State found in their company, and that we desire fully to coöperate in any common arrangements that may include provisions for the aid and care of all sick and wounded soldiers who may be brought to the city from the war.

3. *Resolved*, In view of the prompt and humane action of the physicians and surgeons of this city, that they be invited to send such a delegation to meet and confer with the committee appointed by the meeting, as they may deem proper.

In accordance with, and to carry out the purpose of the Resolutions, the chairman announced the following

COMMITTEE.

Connecticut.
CHARLES GOULD, Esq.,
Gen. PROSPER M. WETMORE,
Col. JOHN H. ALMY, State Agent.

Maine.
DEXTER A. HAWKINS, State Agent,
WILLIAM H. FOGG, Esq.,
Rev. DR. R. D. HITCHCOCK.

Massachusetts.
Col. FRANK E. HOWE, State Agent,
F. E. WELLINGTON, Esq.,
SAMUEL E. LOW, Esq.

New Hampshire.
Hon. BENJAMIN W. BONNEY,
" CHARLES A. PEABODY,
JEREMIAH BURNS, Esq.

Rhode Island.
EDWIN HOYT, Esq.,
WM. J. HOPPIN, Esq.,
Rev. DR. F. VINTON.

Vermont.
E. W. STOUGHTON, Esq.,
Maj. J. A. PULLEN,
JOHN PAINE, Esq.

And subsequently, on motion, the officers of the meeting were added to the committee, viz.:

WILLIAM M. EVARTS, *Massachusetts.*
WILLIAM BOND, *Connecticut.*
MAURICE PERKINS, *Vermont.*

After the adjournment of the meeting, the chairman requested the members of the committee designated, who were present, to remain for the purpose of organizing and making arrangements to carry out the purpose of their appointment.

The names of the committee being called, the following gentlemen were found to be present, viz.:

Messrs.

Gould,	Low,	Burns,
Howe,	Vinton,	Hawkins,
Wetmore,	Pullen,	Hitchcock,
Wellington,	Peabody,	Evarts.
Bond,	Perkins,	

The committee was then called to order, and the following gentlemen were unanimously elected to the offices respectively set to their names, viz.:

William M. Evarts, *Chairman.*
Charles Gould, *Vice-Chairman.*
Samuel E. Low, *Treasurer.*
William Bond, } *Secretaries.*
Maurice Perkins, }

On motion of Mr. Wetmore, it was

Voted, That a committee (of two) on organization be appointed by the Chair, who shall be charged with the particular duty of preparing a written basis of organization for the Association, together with such Articles of Association, By-Laws, and Regulations as they shall deem appropriate, and present the same for the consideration of the committee at their next meeting; whereupon,

Messrs. Wetmore and Peabody were appointed such committee.

On motion of Judge Peabody it was

Voted, That a committee of three be appointed by the Chair, who shall be authorized and requested, in behalf of this body, to communicate with the President, the Secretary of War, and such other members of the National Government as they may deem proper, for the purpose of interchanging views in relation to the relief of sick and wounded soldiers arriving in this city, to the end that mutual co-operation and greater efficiency may be obtained in effecting the purposes of this Association.

Whereupon, Hon. Chas. A. Peabody, Rev. Dr. F. Vinton, and Rev. Dr. Hitchcock were appointed such committee.

After some informal discussion in relation to a suitable building and other accommodations necessary for the purposes of this Association, it was on motion of Col. Howe,

Resolved, That a committee (of three) on location be appointed, who shall be charged with the duty of examining such building or buildings as they may think appropriate for use in administering to the wants, necessities, and comforts of the sick and wounded soldiers arriving in New York, and for the general purposes of this Association, and make a report in relation thereto, at the next meeting of this committee.

Whereupon, Messrs. Howe, Hawkins, and Almy were appointed such committee.

On motion of Rev. Dr. Vinton, it was

Resolved, That the delegations from the several States be requested to communicate directly with the Executive of those States to inquire if it is their desire or intention to repay necessary and certified expenses incurred in ministering to the wants of the soldiers belonging to their respective States.

On motion of Gen. Wetmore, it was

Resolved, That the Committee of Physicians and Surgeons, organized for the purpose of rendering medical assistance to the sick and wounded soldiers, be invited to select three of their number, who shall be members of this Permanent Committee.

On motion of Mr. Gould, it was

Resolved, That this organization be designated as "The Soldiers' Relief Association."

On motion, adjourned, to meet at the Rooms of the Union Defence Committee, No. 30 Pine street, Room 14, on Wednesday, April 2d, at 3 o'clock P. M.

WILLIAM M. EVARTS, *Chairman.*

WILLIAM BOND, } *Secretaries.*
MAURICE PERKINS, }

"NEW ENGLAND SOLDIERS' RELIEF ASSOCIATION."

Wednesday, April 2, 1862.

Pursuant to adjournment the Association met at No. 30 Pine street, Room 14, and was called to order at 3 o'clock p. m., by Mr. Gould, Vice-Chairman.

The following members were present, viz. :

Messrs.

Low,	Almy,	Perkins,
Howe,	Fogg,	Hawkins,
Pullen,	Peabody,	Bond,
Vinton,	Wetmore,	Wellington,
Hitchcock,	Paine,	Burns.
Hoppin,	Gould,	

The following letter from Mr. Edwin Hoyt was presented and read to the meeting :

"NEW YORK, *April* 2, 1862.

"WILLIAM M. EVARTS, Esq., Chairman :

"SIR : I regret that illness prevents me from meeting with the Committee of the Soldiers' Relief Association to-day. This may be the proper occasion for me to correct the erroneous impression that my birth-place was in Rhode Island instead of Connecticut. Deeply as I feel interested in all matters connected with R. I., I should feel out of place in serving on the Committee for that State. I would respectfully suggest the name of my partner, Mr. Nehemiah Knight, of Providence, R. I., who, I feel quite confident, will cheerfully consent to act in my place, and at the same time I would add, that it will afford me pleasure to render him and the

Committee any assistance in my power towards carrying out the good cause.

"Very respectfully,

"Edwin Hoyt."

Mr. Nehemiah Knight, of Rhode Island, was thereupon unanimously elected a member of the Association in place of Mr. Edwin Hoyt, who declined the appointment.

The following letter from Mr. Arad Barrows was then presented and read to the meeting:

"Philadelphia, *April* 1, 1862.

"William M. Evarts, Esq., New York:

"Dear Sir: I notice by the New York *Times* of to-day, that you have been appointed President of an Association formed for the purpose of providing proper attention to the wounded soldiers on their way from the battle-field. On behalf of the Union Volunteer Refreshment Saloon of this city, I respectfully offer the services of our Committee, if they can be of any use to you. We have accommodations at the Hospital for fifty men, but can take a larger number, and give them all care and attention. Hoping to receive an early reply from you, I remain,

"Very truly yours,

"Arad Barrows, Pres't, (per Ritter.)

"N. B.—Please direct to P. O. Box 258."

Whereupon, on motion of Gen. Wetmore, it was

Resolved, That the thanks of this Association be, and they are hereby, cordially tendered to Arad Barrows, Esq., of Philadelphia, and to the committee of which he is the President, in acknowledgment of their humane and friendly offer contained in the letter just read; that the subject-matter in said letter be referred to a committee consisting of Messrs. Almy, Howe, and Hawkins, the agents, respectively, of the States of Connecticut, Massachusetts, and Maine; and that the Secretary notify Mr. Barrows of the action of this committee.

The following letter from Dr. S. Conant Foster was presented and read:

"NEW YORK, *April* 1, 1862.

" W. M. EVARTS, Esq.:

" DEAR SIR: As I was unable to attend the meeting last evening, will you permit me, through you, to tender my professional services to the committee in any way in which they can be made available for the sick and wounded of our armies.

" Very respectfully and truly,
" S. CONANT FOSTER, 24 East 21st st."

Whereupon, on motion of Dr. Vinton, it was

Resolved, That the thanks of this Association be, and they are hereby, tendered to Dr. Foster for his humane and patriotic offer of professional services, and the same are gratefully accepted, and that the Secretary be requested to notify Dr. Foster of the action of this Association.

Rev. Dr. Vinton, from the Committee on Correspondence with the National Government, verbally reported,

That they had communicated in writing to the Secretary of War on the subject-matter of their appointment, and that, during the course of next week, one or more of the members of the committee propose to visit Washington to have a personal interview with the national authorities with reference to this matter.

Mr. Hawkins, from the Committee on Location, verbally reported:

That the building No. 194 Broadway could be rented at the rate of $4,000 per annum, and that Col. Howe would take the first floor and part of the basement, and pay rent therefor at the rate of $2,000 per annum, leaving $2,000 per annum to be paid by this Association for the remainder of the building.

A letter was also read from Dr. Dale, Surgeon-General of the State of Massachusetts, in reference to this building, approving of its interior arrangements and excellent location.

Whereupon, it was unanimously

Resolved, That the Committee on Location be continued, and instructed to rent the building No. 194 Broadway, and prepare the same as speedily as possible for the beneficiaries of this Association.

On motion of Mr. Hawkins, it was

Voted, That a Finance Committee be appointed, to consist of one member from each State.

Whereupon, Messrs.

FOGG, of Maine,
PEABODY, of New Hampshire,
PAINE, of Vermont,
WELLINGTON, of Massachusetts,
KNIGHT, of Rhode Island, and
R. H. McCURDY, of Connecticut,

were appointed such committee.

On motion, it was

Voted, That Mr. Low, the Treasurer of this Association, be added to said committee, and be, ex-officio, the Chairman thereof.

On motion of Gen. Wetmore,

Rev. Dr. H. W. Bellows and Rev. Dr. Samuel Osgood were unanimously elected members of this Association.

The Committee on Organization made a verbal report, and asked leave to defer making the Report in writing until the next meeting of the Association, which was granted.

On motion of Mr. Gould, it was

Voted, That the Secretary divide this General Committee into five sub-committees, exclusive of the several State agents, to form visiting committees for the purpose of receiving, visiting, and attending to the wounded and disabled soldiers as they shall, from time to time, arrive in the city ; such sub-committees to coöperate with the State agents and medical attendants, each committee to serve one week, and to have the powers of substitution and of increasing their numbers.

Mr. Burns, on behalf of the proprietors of the Astor House, tendered to this Association the gratuitous use of a room or rooms in their hotel for the purpose of holding the meetings of the Association at any time they may desire to make such use of them.

Whereupon, it was

Voted, That the thanks of this Association be, and they are hereby, tendered to the proprietors of the Astor House for their liberal and generous offer.

General Wetmore made a verbal statement, setting forth some of the many acts of charity and kindness rendered by the proprietors of the Astor House to New England troops passing through New York, and particularly by Mr. Charles Stetson and family to the wounded and sick soldiers who have been brought to this city, and thereupon offered the following

PREAMBLE AND RESOLUTION.

Whereas, this Association has been informed of the many acts of Christian charity, sympathy, and kindness shown by Charles A. Stetson, Esq., and family, to the wounded, sick, and suffering soldiers who have passed through this city on their way to their homes from the seat of war.

And, whereas, it is the duty, as well as the pleasure of this Association to recognize and acknowledge such acts of disinterested benevolence and patriotism, therefore,

Resolved, unanimously, that this committee tender their sincere thanks to General Stetson and the members of his family for their kind attentions to the sick and wounded soldiers who have passed through New York on their way to their homes.

Resolved, That the Secretary cause this Preamble and Resolution to be engrossed, signed by the officers of this Association, and sent to Mr. Stetson.

On motion, adjourned to meet at this place on Thursday April 3, at half-past three o'clock P. M.

WILLIAM BOND, *Secretary.*

"NEW ENGLAND SOLDIERS' RELIEF ASSOCIATION."

ADJOURNED MEETING.

THURSDAY, *April* 3, 1862.

Pursuant to adjournment, the Association met at No. 30 Pine street, Room No. 14, and was called to order at half-past three o'clock P. M., by Mr. Gould, Vice-Chairman.

The following members of the Association were present:

Messrs.

Fogg,	Paine,	Low,	Wetmore,
Peabody,	Perkins,	Vinton,	Almy,
Burns,	Howe,	Knight,	Bond,
Pullen,	Wellington,	Gould,	Bellows.

The Secretary read the minutes of previous meetings, which were approved, and the proceedings were unanimously confirmed.

The Committee on Organization reported in writing through General Wetmore, Chairman, and presented a basis of organization, which was read and discussed, section by section.

After a considerable discussion by Messrs. Bellows, Vinton, Wetmore, Peabody, Almy, Paine, Howe, Burns, and others, upon the subject-matter of Article 1, relating to a name for this Association, the Article was amended by filling the blank left by the Committee with the words " New England Soldiers' Relief Association."

The Report of the Committee was then accepted, and the basis of organization, as amended and reported com-

plete by the Committee, was adopted, and ordered to be recorded with the minutes.

PREAMBLE.

This Association, representing the sons of New England
resident in the city of New York appointed in public meeting for the purpose of forming an association to aid and
care for the sick and wounded soldiers passing through the
city of New York on their way to or from the war, do
hereby adopt the following

PLAN OF ORGANIZATION:

First. The name of this Association shall be " New
England Soldiers' Relief Association."

Second. The officers of this Association shall be a Chairman, a Vice-Chairman, Treasurer, Corresponding Secretary,
and two Recording Secretaries.

Third. The Association shall hold their meetings for the
transaction of business by adjournment, or whenever called
together by order of the Chairman or Vice-Chairman, or of
any three members of the Association.

Fourth. The Chairman or Vice-Chairman shall preside
at all meetings, and they shall be governed by the usual
rules of order. In case of the absence of both these officers,
the Association may appoint a Chairman pro tempore.

Fifth. The funds of the Association shall be provided
by voluntary contribution, and shall in all cases be paid
into the hands of the Treasurer, who shall keep a record of
all receipts, and shall disburse them only on bills duly certified by one of the State agents, and approved by the
Chairman or Vice-Chairman. The Treasurer shall report
the state of the finances whenever he may deem it desirable.
and whenever requested to do so by the Association. He
shall be, ex-officio, a member and Chairman of the Finance
Committee, when the same shall be appointed.

Sixth. The Corresponding Secretary shall conduct the
correspondence and preserve copies thereof in a volume to
be devoted to that purpose for the use of this Association.

Seventh. The Recording Secretaries shall record the proceedings of the Association in a volume provided for that purpose, and be present at each meeting. They shall keep record of the attendance of the members, and shall call the roll of members promptly at the hour named for the meeting.

Eighth. The Secretary shall select from this Association five committees, (excluding the several State agents,) to form visiting committees for the purpose of receiving, disposing of, visiting, and attending to the wounded or disabled soldiers as they shall, from time to time, arrive in the city; such committees to coöperate with the State agents and medical attendants; each committee to serve one week, and to have the powers of substitution and of increasing their numbers at pleasure; and the Recording Secretary shall give due written notice to each member of the committee of his turn.

Ninth. This Association shall have power to call general meetings of the sons of New England at such times as may be deemed proper, in order to submit to their consideration the action and plans of the Association, and to solicit their aid and advice in promoting the objects of this Association, namely, the tender care of volunteer soldiers who may have been disabled in the camp, in battle, and on the march to or from the seat of war.

Tenth. These articles may be altered or added to at any meeting by a vote of a majority of the Association present, notice of the alteration or addition having been given at a previous meeting.

Eleventh. At any meeting of this Association, the number of nine shall constitute a quorum for the transaction of business.

The Committee on Location made a verbal report, stating that the building rented for the use of this Association would be ready on the fifth day of April.

Rev. Dr. Vinton then offered, and Judge Peabody seconded, the following resolution :

Resolved, That Col. Frank E. Howe be appointed Superintendent of the rooms and offices provided for the use of this Association, which was unanimously adopted.

Mr. Gould then read the following letter from Governor Sprague, of Rhode Island, which was ordered to be recorded with the minutes.

"STATE OF RHODE ISLAND, &c., }
"EXECUTIVE DEPARTMENT. }
"PROVIDENCE, *April* 2, 1862.

"DEAR SIR : I have the pleasure to acknowledge the receipt of your favor of the 29th ult., communicating a copy of Resolutions passed at a meeting of the New Englanders.'

"Be pleased to accept my thanks for your complimentary action. We are proud to be New Englanders, and to work under that honored name.

"I am, very truly, your obedient servant,
"WM. SPRAGUE.
"To CHAS. GOULD, Esq., Secretary, &c."

Rev. Dr. Bellows, on behalf of the President and Faculty of the Thirteenth Street Medical College, offered for the free use of this Association a ward in their Hospital with accommodations and medical attendance for one hundred of the beneficiaries of this Association.

Whereupon, it was unanimously

Resolved, That the thanks of this Association be, and they are, tendered to the President and Faculty of the Thirteenth Street Medical College, for their liberal, humane, and patriotic offer, which is gratefully accepted and referred to Messrs. Hawkins, Almy, and Howe, to confer with them more particularly in reference thereto.

Dr. Perkins having in behalf of Dr. T. M. Cheeseman tendered his professional services to this Association, it was, on motion of Mr. Pullen,

Resolved, That the thanks of this Association be, and they are hereby, tendered to Dr. Cheeseman for his humane and patriotic offer of professional services, and the same are gratefully accepted, and that the Secretary be requested to notify Dr. Cheeseman of the action of this Association.

The Secretary, Mr. William Bond, submitted the following

REPORT.

The Secretary respectfully submits:

That, acting under the resolution authorizing him to subdivide this General Committee for certain purposes in said resolution specified, he has subdivided this General Committee into three sub-committees, leaving two to be hereafter designated, and that said sub-committees are constituted as follows:

Messrs. Hitchcock,
    Wellington,   } For the week ending
    Pullen,   *April* 10.
    Gould,

    Vinton,
    Peabody,   } For the week ending
    Low,   *April* 17.
 , Wetmore,

    Paine,
    Burns,   } For the week ending
    Hoppin,   *April* 24.
    Fogg,

Which report was unanimously adopted, and the Secretary was requested to notify the gentlemen above designated, in relation thereto.

On motion of Rev. Dr. Vinton, it was unanimously

Resolved, That the officers of this Association be, and they are hereby, appointed a committee to carry out the object and purposes of the resolutions passed at the Fifth Avenue Hotel meeting in reference to inviting the coöperation of other bodies and associations with this Association.

On motion of Gen. Wetmore, Mr. William H. L. Barnes was elected Corresponding Secretary of this Association.

On motion, Messrs. Low, Gould, and Bond were appointed a Committee on Printing, with instructions to provide such Books, Printed Blanks, &c., as they may deem necessary.

Rev. Dr. Bellows, on behalf of the Sanitary Commission

tendered to this Association, hospital stores, garments, medicines, and such other articles as may conduce to the wants and comforts of the beneficiaries of this Association, the same to be furnished at any time at their depot on the requisition of the proper representatives of this Association.

Whereupon, Rev. Dr. Vinton offered the following preamble and resolution, which were unanimously adopted :

Whereas, The Sanitary Commission, by their President, Rev. Dr. Bellows, has made offer to this Association of hospital stores, garments, medicines, and other useful and necessary articles, therefore

Resolved, That the thanks of this Association be, and they are hereby, tendered to the Sanitary Commission for their considerate offer, which is thankfully accepted.

On motion, adjourned to meet at the Astor House on Friday, April 4, 1862, at $3\frac{1}{2}$ o'clock P. M.

WILLIAM BOND, *Secretary.*

2

"NEW ENGLAND SOLDIERS' RELIEF ASSOCIATION."

ADJOURNED MEETING.

FRIDAY, *April 4th*, 1862.

The Association met pursuant to adjournment, at half past three P. M., at room No. 41, Astor House.

The Chairman and Vice-Chairman being absent, on motion of Rev. Dr. Vinton, Gen. P. M. Wetmore was unanimously elected Chairman *pro tempore*.

The following members were present, viz. :

Messrs. Hawkins, Pullen, Wellington, Vinton, Wetmore, Barnes, Peabody, Gould, Burns, Howe, Low, Knight, Almy, Hitchcock, Bond.

The minutes of the last meeting were read by the Corresponding Secretary.

The Chairman suggested that he had observed a discrepancy between the minutes and the by-laws embodied in them as respected the title of this body. In the one it was described as a Committee, and in the other as an Association. He thought this the proper time to determine whether it was an Association or a Committee of an Association. After discussion by Rev. Dr. Vinton, Mr. Hawkins, and others, on motion of Rev. Dr. Vinton, the minutes were amended so as to read " Association," wherever the word " Committee" occurs.

The minutes as amended were then unanimously approved.

On motion of Mr. Hawkins, the Corresponding Secretary was directed to inform all members of the Committee of their election, and to obtain information whether they intended to serve.

The Chairman directed the Secretary to read a communication received by the Association from George Bliss, jr., A. D. C., and Col. Commanding N. Y. Depot of Volunteers, which was read, as follows:

OFFICE OF COMMANDANT OF DEPOT }
OF VOLUNTEERS,

NEW YORK, *April* 4, 1862.

CHARLES GOULD, Esq., *Vice-Chairman, &c.*:

DEAR SIR: I beg to inform you that, on behalf of the State of New York, I am engaged in fitting up the southern portion of the Park Barracks on Broadway, as a temporary receiving hospital, for the sick and wounded volunteers arriving in this city. It is intended to provide at once one hundred beds, and to arrange so that as many more can be added at a few hours' notice, but the building is large enough to accommodate many more than this if needed.

The Association of Physicians and Surgeons of New York and Brooklyn, (represented by Dr. Wood at the meeting at which your Committee was appointed,) will take medical charge of the patients.

In the same spirit which has led the State of New York to throw the Park Barracks open freely to the use of all regiments and soldiers arriving in this city, it is both my duty and my pleasure to state these facts to the Committee over which you preside, and to express the hope that they will find it consistent with their views of duty and propriety, to coöperate in this effort to care for all sick and wounded volunteers.

I may be allowed to add that the Park Barracks seem to me better adapted than any other building I know of, to answer the purpose your Committee have in view—the reception and care for a few hours of sick and wounded men.

I need hardly add in behalf of the State, that I shall cordially coöperate with your Committee in laboring for a common end. My desire is to see one systematic and efficient organization at work, representing all the States whose sick and wounded men are likely to arrive here, and caring for all alike.

Such accommodations as your Committee may desire in addition to those now preparing, will be readily furnished you at the Park Barracks without expense; or, if your Committee desire it, arrangements can easily be made for sharing the expense.

May I beg the favor of an early answer in order that, if you wish it, your views may be consulted in the fitting up of the Barracks?

I am, sir,

Your obedient servant,

GEO. BLISS, jr.,

A. D. C., and Colonel Commanding
N. Y. Depot of Volunteers.

Whereupon, Rev. Dr. Vinton offered the following resolution, which was unanimously adopted:

Resolved, That this Association cordially reciprocates the offer of Col. Bliss, A. D. C. and Col. Commanding N. Y. Depot of Volunteers, to coöperate with this Association in the care of sick and wounded soldiers returning from the seat of war to their homes.

Resolved, That the Secretary inform Col. Bliss, A. D. C., &c., that the building occupied by the New England Soldiers' Relief Association, 194 Broadway, is open at all hours for the admission of any disabled soldiers returning from the war.

The following letter was then presented and read from Dr. John H. Griscom:

42 EAST 29TH ST., *April* 4, 1862.

MY DEAR SIR: Should the Committee of the Sons of New England desire any counsel in relation to the hygienic or medical arrangements, contemplated for the reception and care of the sick and wounded soldiers *in transitu* through this city, it will afford me great pleasure to render any assistance in my power.

The sick volunteers now in the New York Hospital, occupy some portion of my time at present, but I will gladly give any required attention in aid of the benevolent labors of your organization.

Very respectfully,

JNO. H. GRISCOM.

CHAS. GOULD, Esq.

Whereupon, on motion of Col. Howe, it was

Resolved, That the thanks of this Association be, and they are hereby, tendered to Dr. Griscom for his humane and patriotic offer of professional services, and the same are gratefully accepted, and that the Secretary be requested to notify Dr. Griscom of the action of this Association.

Gen. Wetmore, on behalf of Dr. A. K. Gardner, having tendered his profesional services to this Association, it was, on motion of Rev. Dr. Vinton,

Resolved, That the thanks of this Association be and they are hereby, tendered to Dr. Gardner for his humane and patriotic offer of professional services, and the same are gratefully accepted, and that the Secretary be requested to notify Dr. Gardner of the action of this Association.

The Chairman suggested that it was necessary to fill the blank in Section Eleven of the Plan of Organization, declaring what number should constitute a quorum; and, after some discussion, on motion of Rev. Dr. Vinton, it was resolved that nine should be inserted in the said section, so that nine members of the Association should constitute a quorum thereof.

The Chairman then announced the organization of the Association to be complete.

Mr. Hawkins moved the appointment of a committee of three, to prepare a suitable book for the enrolling of the members of the Association, and preserving a record of their respective offerings in aid of the Association. Carried.

The Chairman appointed as such committee Messrs. Hawkins, Vinton, and Knight.

On motion of Mr. Knight, the Corresponding Secretary was directed to prepare and cause to be printed, in a compendious form, 1,000 copies of the Plan of Organization of the Association, together with a list of its officers, and a description of the building occupied by the Association.

On motion of Col. Howe, the State Agents were appointed a committee to procure a suitable flag-staff and flag for the Association building, 194 Broadway.

On motion of Dr. Vinton, the State Agents were appointed a committee to procure suitable books for recording the names, &c., of all visitors to the Association, and also a book for recording the names, residences, and other facts of interest, of all beneficiaries of the Association.

The Treasurer, being called on to report, stated that there had as yet been no meeting of the Finance Committee, and he had nothing to report.

On motion of Mr. Almy, seconded by Col. Howe, it was unanimously

Resolved, That R. H. McCurdy, Esq., be, and he is hereby, elected a member of this Association.

Col. Howe proposed Hon. R. J. Andrews, Surveyor of the port of New York, as a member of the Association, which was seconded by Mr. Pullen, whereupon it was unanimously

Resolved, That Hon. R. J. Andrews be, and he is hereby, elected a member of this Association.

Resolved, That the Secretary notify Messrs. McCurdy and Andrews of their respective elections, and invite their attendance at future deliberations of the Association.

Dr. Vinton gave notice that, at the next meeting of the Association, he should move to amend the by-laws by adding thereto a provision for the election of honorary members of the Association, who should not be resident in the State of New York.

Mr. Hawkins gave notice that, at the next meeting of the Association, he should move to amend the by-laws by adding thereto a provision for membership of the Association whereby all New Englanders, or descendants of New Englanders, residing in New York, may become members thereof by enrolling their names and residence in the book of members.

Col. Howe informed the Association, that Messrs. Stetson had provided a temperance collation in an adjoining room, to which attention was specially invited.

On motion of Col. Howe, a recess was taken.

After the collation Mr. Charles Gould gave notice that, at the next meeting of the Association, he should move to amend the Plan of Organization by adding thereto the following section :

Any member, living in the city, who shall absent himself from three successive meetings of which he shall have been notified, without excuse, shall be deemed, *ipso facto*, to have resigned his office, and his connection with the Association shall thenceforward cease.

On motion of Col. Howe, it was unanimously

Resolved, That the thanks of this Association and of each individual here present be, and they are hereby, gratefully tendered to the proprietors of the Astor House for the characteristic liberality which they have this day shown to this Association.

On motion of Rev. Dr. Vinton, the Association adjourned to meet on Tuesday evening, the 8th instant, at 8 o'clock P. M., at the Fifth Avenue Hotel.

WM. H. L. BARNES,

Cor. Sec. and Sec'y pro tem.

"NEW ENGLAND SOLDIERS' RELIEF ASSOCIATION."

ADJOURNED MEETING OF THE ASSOCIATION.

Tuesday, April 8, 1862.

Pursuant to adjournment, the Association met at the Fifth Avenue Hotel, and was called to order at 8 o'clock p. m., by Mr. Gould, Vice-Chairman.

The following members were present, viz. :

DEXTER A. HAWKINS, Esq., State Agent,
WILLIAM H. FOGG, Esq.,
Rev. R. D. HITCHCOCK, D.D.,
Hon. BENJ. W. BONNEY,
Hon. CHARLES A. PEABODY,
Maj. J. A. PULLEN,
JOHN PAINE, Esq.,
WILLIAM BOND, Esq.,
Dr. MAURICE PERKINS,

Col. FRANK E. HOWE, State Agent,
F. E. WELLINGTON, Esq.,
SAMUEL E. LOW, Esq.,
NEHEMIAH KNIGHT, Esq.,
Col. JOHN H. ALMY, State Agent,
Gen. PROSPER M. WETMORE,
CHARLES GOULD, Esq.,
Rev. SAMUEL OSGOOD, D. D.,
SAMUEL W. BRIDGHAM, Esq.

The Secretary read the minutes of the last meeting, which were approved, and the proceedings were unanimously confirmed.

Gen. Wetmore called up the amendment to the Plan of Organization, which Rev. Dr. Vinton gave notice at the last meeting he should offer for the consideration and action of this body. The amendment, after some discussion, was passed in the following words :

"Section 12. This Association shall be empowered to elect such honorary members from time to time as may be deemed expedient.

The amendment offered by Mr. Hawkins, of which he had given notice at a previous meeting, was then brought up, and was discussed by Mr. Hawkins, Gen. Wetmore, Judge Bonney, and Judge Peabody, at some length ; after which discussion the amendment was withdrawn, and the following resolution, offered by Mr. H wkins and seconded by Rev. Dr. Hitchcock, was unanimously adopted :

Resolved, That all natives of New England resident in the State of New York, desirous of coöperating with this Association, be invited to enroll their names and residences in the Register of the Association, and make whatever offering they may be disposed to make to the funds of the Association.

The following letter from Rev. Dr. Bellows, President of the Sanitary Commission, was then presented, and read to the meeting :

U. S. SANITARY COMMISSION, }
NEW YORK, *April* 8, 1862. }

My DEAR Mr. GOULD : A meeting of the Executive Committee of the Sanitary Commission, at the very hour of your meeting this evening, makes my presence impossible at the session of the New England Soldiers' Relief Association.

Being anxious, however, to know what measure of dependence you are going to place upon the stores of the Woman's Central Association, (one branch of the Sanitary Commission in this city,) I have requested my friend Mr. Bridgham, the active Committee man *on supplies*, in that body, to wait on you, to learn what you may now want, and are likely to want from us. As we are constantly sending off our supplies to distant points, we do not wish to retain here more than is needful, while we are most anxious at the same time to retain all that is needful to meet the requirements of your highly respected body.

Please receive Mr. Bridgham in my name, and consider him as an official visitor from the Sanitary Commission.

Of course he does not expect to intrude upon your Committee meeting ; but waits your orders, and such reception as your rules and wishes may allow.

Respectfully yours,

HENRY W. BELLOWS,
Pres. of the U. S. San. Com.

After the reading of the letter, on motion, Mr. Samuel W. Bridgham was unanimously elected a member of the Association.

It being announced by Col. Howe, that Rev. Mr. Henry, Chaplain of the United States Hospital at Annapolis, was then in an adjoining room, he was on motion invited to meet with the Association, and Col. Howe was appointed a special committee to procure his attendance, which duty was immediately performed.

The amendment offered by Mr. Gould, of which he had given notice at a previous meeting, was then brought up, and, after discussion, was adopted in the following words :

Section 13. Any member being in the city, who shall, without excuse, absent himself from three successive meetings, (of which he shall have been notified,) shall be deemed, *ipso facto*, to have resigned his office, and his connection with the Association shall thenceforward cease.

The following letter from the Assistant Adjutant-General of Rhode Island, was then read, and the Secretary instructed to communicate the information desired :

STATE OF RHODE ISLAND, &c.,
ADJUTANT GENERAL'S OFFICE,
PROVIDENCE, *5th April*, 1862.

Secretary Soldiers' Relief Association :

SIR : I am directed by his Excellency the Governor, to say that Rhode Island will cordially unite with the other States, in giving support to your organization.

He would be very glad if you would communicate to this department, the plans of the Association, &c.

I am, very respectfully, your obedient servant,

AUG. HOPPIN,
Assistant Adjutant-General.

WM. BOND, Esq.

On the nomination of Gen. Wetmore, seconded by Judge Bonney, the following gentlemen were unanimously elected honorary members of this Association, and the Secretary was requested to notify them of their election :

His Excellency, Governor ANDREW,
of Massachusetts.

"   "   Governor SPRAGUE,
of Rhode Island.

"   "   Governor BUCKINGHAM,
of Connecticut.

"   "   Governor HOLBROOK,
of Vermont.

"   "   Governor WASHBURNE,
of Maine.

"   "   Governor BERRY,
of New Hampshire.

"   "   Governor MORGAN,
of New York.

Gen. Wetmore, after a few remarks, nominated Col. George Bliss, jr., commanding New York Depot of Volunteers, as a member of this Association, which nomination was seconded by Col. Howe, and carried unanimously, and the Secretary requested to notify Col. Bliss of his election.

The following communication was then presented and read :

We, the undersigned, place our professional services entirely at the order of the New England Soldiers' Relief Association, holding ourselves ready to attend to the wants of the wounded soldiers arriving in this city, at any hour of the day or night.

A. K. GARDNER, M. D., 144 East 13th st.

W. R. DONAGHE, M. D., 102 4th Avenue.

J. E. STEELE, M. D., Irving Place.

J. P. GARRISH, M. D., 40 West 21st st.

HORACE GREEN, M. D., 12 Clinton Place.

GEO. B. BOUTON, 44 East 11th st.

J. C. KENNEDY, Duane st.

Whereupon, on motion of Rev. Dr. Osgood, it was unanimously

Resolved, That the thanks of this Association be, and they are hereby, tendered to Drs. Gardner, Donaghe, Steele, Garrish, Green, Bouton, and Kennedy, for their humane

and patriotic offer of professional services, and the same are
gratefully accepted ; and that the Secretary be requested
to notify those gentlemen severally of the action of this Association.

The Secretary, Mr. William Bond, submitted the following :

The Secretary respectfully submits—

That, acting under the Eighth Section of the Plan of
Organization, which reads as follows :

Eighth. The Secretary shall select from this Association
five committees, (excluding the several State Agents,) to
form Visiting Committees for the purpose of receiving, disposing of, visiting, and attending to the wounded or disabled soldiers as they shall, from time to time, arrive in the
city ; such committees to coöperate with the State Agents
and medical attendants ; each committee to serve one week,
and to have the powers of substitution, and of increasing
their numbers at pleasure ; and the Recording Secretary
shall give due notice to each member of the committee of
his turn—

He has selected the following

VISITING COMMITTEES :

For the Week ending April 17th.

Rev. Francis Vinton, D. D., Hon. Chas. A. Peabody,
Samuel E. Low, Esq., Gen. Prosper M. Wetmore.

For the Week ending April 24th.

John Paine, Esq., Jeremiah Burns, Esq.,
William J. Hoppin, Esq., William H. Fogg, Esq.

For the Week ending May 1.

Rev. Samuel Osgood, D. D., R. H. McCurdy, Esq.,
Nehemiah Knight, Esq., Hon. Benj. W. Bonney.

For the Week ending May 8th.

Rev. R. D. Hitchcock, D. D., F. E. Wellington, Esq.,
Maj. J. A. Pullen, Wm. H. L. Barnes, Esq.

WILLIAM M. EVARTS, Esq.,   Rev. FRANCIS VINTON, D. D.,
SAMUEL E. LOW, Esq.,   CHARLES GOULD, Esq.

Also that due notice has been sent to each member of the committees designated.

WILLIAM BOND, *Secretary.*

Which report was unanimously accepted.

Rev. Dr. Hitchcock, after a few prefatory remarks, read a letter which he had received, in which the writer, on the part of herself and others, tendered their services in any way that they could be rendered available in coöperation with this Association in ministering to the wants, necessities, and comforts of the sick and wounded soldiers who shall arrive in this city, and suggesting the plan of an auxiliary association of women to be organized and conducted under the supervision of this Association, in order that the purposes of this humane charity may be carried out with greater system and efficiency.

The subject-matter referred to in the letter was discussed by Rev. Dr. Hitchcock, Rev. Dr. Osgood, Mr. Bond, Judge Peabody, Col. Howe, and others; after which discussion the following resolutions were offered by Mr. Bond, seconded by Judge Peabody, and unanimously adopted:

Resolved, That this Association, recognizing the eminent propriety of rendering such services, gratefully accept the offer made through Rev. Dr. Hitchcock, of the assistance of an Association of women in promoting the objects of this Association as declared in the basis of organization, namely, "the tender care of volunteer soldiers who may be or may become disabled in the camp, in battle, or on the march to or from the seat of war."

Resolved, That a committee of three, of which the Rev. Dr. Hitchcock shall be the Chairman, be appointed with full power to initiate, and on behalf of this organization to perfect, a plan by which the assistance and services of an auxiliary association of women may be made available in accomplishing the purposes of this Association,—such committee to make a report in writing of their action, under this resolution, to the next meeting of this Association.

Whereupon, Rev. Dr. Hitchcock, Rev. Dr. Osgood, and Col. Frank E. Howe, Superintendent, &c., were appointed such committee.

On motion of Col. Howe, it was

Voted, That the officers of this Association be requested to officially notify Lieut.-Col. A. B. Eaton, Assistant Commissary-General of Subsistence, U. S. A., of the organization and purpose of this Association, and request from him such official coöperation as he may deem consistent with the regulations of his department.

Col. Howe announced that he had received official information from the Executive authorities of Rhode Island, expressing their cordial sympathy and desire to coöperate with this Association in carrying out its benevolent purposes.

Col. Howe announced that he had received a communication from His Excellency, Gov. Andrew, expressing his gratification at the organization of this Association, and signifying his intention to place at their disposal an ambulance to be used for the comfortable transportation of the sick and wounded soldiers through the city.

Col. Almy stated to the meeting, that he had recently seen His Excellency, Governor Buckingham, of Connecticut, who had desired him to express his warm appreciation of the objects of this organization, and on behalf of the State, his thanks for their thoughtful and considerate kindness in making provision for the sick and wounded Connecticut soldiers. He also asked permission to be allowed to contribute personally to the treasury of the Association the sum of one hundred dollars.

The Committee on Location asked for instruction in relation to certain details connected with the fitting up of the building No. 194 Broadway, which after discussion was referred to the Committee with power to determine

On motion of Mr. Knight, it was

Voted, That the Finance Committee be authorized and requested to perfect the details connected with the lease of the premises No. 194 Broadway.

Mr. Bridgham, on behalf of the Sanitary Commission, made some remarks in reference to the matters referred to in the letter of Rev. Dr. Bellows, previously read.

Whereupon, on motion, it was

Resolved, That the General Superintendent, Col. Frank E. Howe, with Messrs. Almy and Hawkins, State Agents, be appointed a committee to confer with the Sanitary Commission in regard to the inquiries and suggestions contained in the communication of Rev. Dr. Bellows, President, &c., and to determine the action of this Association in relation thereto.

Rev. Mr. Henry being called upon, addressed the meeting, and made some interesting statements regarding the hospital at Annapolis, and also gave the benefit of his observation and experience with soldiers, in furtherance of the general purposes of this Association.

On motion, adjourned to meet at No. 194 Broadway, on Tuesday, April 15, at 7½ p. m.

WILLIAM BOND, *Secretary.*

•

"NEW ENGLAND SOLDIERS' RELIEF ASSOCIATION."

ADJOURNED MEETING OF THE ASSOCIATION.

Tuesday, April 15, 1862.

Pursuant to adjournment, the Association met at the Association Building, No. 194 Broadway.

Present, Messrs.

HAWKINS,	FOGG,	HITCHCOCK,
BONNEY,	PEABODY,	BURNS,
PULLEN,	PAINE,	HOWE,
WELLINGTON,	LOW,	KNIGHT,
HOPPIN,	ALMY,	WETMORE,
GOULD,	BRIDGHAM,	OSGOOD,
	PERKINS.	

The Chairman and Vice-Chairman being absent, the meeting was called to order, at half-past 7 o'clock, by Gen. P. M. Wetmore, upon whose nomination,

Judge Bonney was called to the Chair.

The minutes of the last preceding meeting were read and approved.

The Treasurer of the Association, Mr. Low, from the Finance Committee, made a verbal report, that the Committee has met with marked and gratifying success in their labors; that, although the printed subscription lists were only ready for use on Friday night last, yet the lists handed in to-night show subscriptions to the amount of $2,455; and the Committee has no doubt of obtaining, without any difficulty, the whole amount that may be required.

The report was accepted, and received with acclamation.

The Vice-Chairman, Mr. Gould, having entered, took the chair at the request of Judge Bonney.

Rev. Dr. Hitchcock, from the Committee appointed at the last meeting to arrange a plan of coöperation with the proposed Auxiliary Association of Women, reported :

That the Committee had succeeded in securing the co-operation of thirty ladies, under the following arrangement :

"THE WOMEN'S AUXILIARY COMMITTEE

OF THE

NEW ENGLAND SOLDIERS' RELIEF ASSOCIATION,"

Is divided into five weekly committees, and they are expected to hold themselves in readiness to attend at the Association Building, No. 194 Broadway, during their respective weeks, upon due notice being given.

For the Week ending April 24.

Mrs. John Paine, No. 140 Fifth Avenue.
Miss Jane S. Woolsey, No. 8 Brevoort Place.
Mrs. R. D. Hitchcock, No. 149 East Twelfth Street.
Mrs. H. B. Smith, No. 34 East Twenty-fifth Street.
Mrs. Dr. Gurdon Buck, No. 121 Tenth Street.
Mrs. George S. Robbins, No. 39 East Twenty-third St.

For the Week ending May 1.

Mrs. Samuel Osgood, No. 154 West Eleventh Street.
Mrs. G. Winthrop Gray, No. 32 Washington Square.
Mrs. J. W. Post, No. 79 West Tenth Street.
Mrs. A. Brookes, No. 32 West Thirty-first Street.
Mrs. A. C. Richards, Fort Washington.
Mrs. W. G. Sterling, No. 32 West Thirty-third Street.

For the Week ending May 8.

Mrs. Charles Gould, No. 5 East Twenty-sixth Street.
Mrs. Andrew Wesson, Madison Av. cor. Fortieth St.
Miss Gilman, No. 74 East Twenty-seventh Street.
Miss McCurdy, No. 10 East Fourteenth Street.
Mrs. M. O. Roberts, No. 118 Fifth Avenue.
Miss Annie Potts, No. 27 Fifth Avenue.

34

For the Week ending May 15.

Mrs. Frank E. Howe, No. 94 East Twenty-first Street.
Mrs. Washington Hunt, Albemarle Hotel.
Mrs. H. W. Hubbell, No. 75 East Twenty-third Street.
Mrs. E. V. Haughwout, No. 92 East Twenty-first Street.
Mrs. E. W. Stoughton, cor. Fifth Av. and 17th Street.
Mrs. Fred'k Swan, No. 2 East Thirty-fifth Street.

For the Week ending May 22.

Mrs. R. R. Booth, No. 121 Ninth Street.
Mrs. Hilliard, No. 410 West Twenty-third Street.
Mrs. G. Kissell, Staten Island.
Mrs. George Brown, No. 29 Washington Square.
Mrs. Henry V. Poor, No. 81 St. Mark's Place.
Miss Post, No. 11 West Seventeenth Street.

And the Secretary was requested to cause to be printed 100 copies of the foregoing list of the committees of ladies, to be used and distributed under the direction of the Committee.

Col. Howe, Superintendent, reported:

That Drs. Buck and Stone, from the Committee of Physicians and Surgeons, have examined the internal arrangements of the Association Building, and expressed with pleasure their approval of the location of the building, its fitting up and interior accommodations, and more particularly its excellent ventilation.

That Dr. Buck has since informed the Superintendent that he has reported these facts to the New York Surgical Aid Association, which he represents; that that body is ready to coöperate with this Association, proposing to send a medical clerk to be in constant attendance here; that Dr. Buck has given directions for certain tables for surgical operations; also that Dr. Buck has donated to this Association a case of medicines.

In this connection, the following note from Dr. Buck

was presented, and ordered, with the accompanying paper, to be entered on the minutes:

"NEW YORK, *April* 14, 1862.

"WM. M. EVARTS, Esq., *Chairman N. E. S. Relief Association:*

"DEAR SIR: I beg leave to inclose herewith an extract from the proceedings of the N. York Surgical Aid Association, which you will please submit to the New England Soldiers' Relief Association. Hoping that our proposition may result in the harmonious coöperation of both Associations,

"I remain, very respectfully and truly, yours, &c.,
"GURDON BUCK,
"*Chairman Ex. Com., &c.*, 121 *Tenth st.*"

"At a meeting of the New York Surgical Aid Association's Executive Committee, held on the 10th April, 1862, a communication from the New England Soldiers' Relief Association was submitted and read. Thereupon it was

"*Resolved*, That though this Association deem it inexpedient, and respectfully decline to send representatives from their own body to be members of the Permanent Committee of the New England Soldiers' Relief Association, they are desirous, and hereby offer to render all necessary professional services to the sick and wounded soldiers under the jurisdiction of the New England Association, provided arrangements mutually satisfactory can be made for accomplishing the object.

"*Resolved*, That Doctors Buck and Stone be appointed a Committee of Conference, to communicate the above resolution, and with power to carry its provisions into effect.

"GURDON BUCK, M. D.,
"*Chairman Exec. Committee.*
"CHAS. K. BRIDDON, M. D.,
"*Sec. Exec. Committee.*"

Col. Howe reported further that he had received from Dr. R. S. Satterlee, Assistant Medical Purveyor's office, New York, the following invoice of Hospital Bedding, &c., and the donation of sundry articles from several generous friends:

Invoice of Hospital Bedding, &c., furnished to Col. Frank E. Howe, Superintendent Soldiers' Relief Association :

> "ARMY MED. PURVEYOR'S OFFICE,}
> "NEW YORK, *April* 9, 1862. {

BOOKS.

	No.
Hospital Registers, . .	1

BEDDING, ETC.

Bedsteads, iron, .	150
Bed sacks, . .	150
Blankets, woollen, . . .	150
Coverlets, . .	150
Pillow Cases, . .	300
" Ticks, . .	150
Sheets, muslin, . . .	300
Towels, ...	100
Cups, tin, ...	24
Pots, Coffee and Tea,	12
Litters, Hand, . . .	4
Chair Close Stool, .'	1
Boxes, Packing, ...	1

> R. I. SATTERLEE,
> *Purveyor and Sec.*

And also from the United States Sanitary Commission the following list of articles :

33 Quilts.	30 Pair Drawers.
50 Woollen Shirts.	25 Pair Slippers.
50 Pair Woollen Socks.	100 Pillows.
30 Shirts.	30 Cushions for wounded.
150 Towels.	16 Jars Currant Jelly.

1 box containing a supply of Lint, Bandages, Adhesive Plaster, old Cotton and Linen, and other appliances for the wounded.

The following letters were presented, and ordered to be placed on the minutes :

"Office of Asst. Com. Gen. Subsistence,
"New York, *April* 14, 1862.
"Charles Gould, Esq.,
" *Vice-Chairman N. E. S. Relief Association:*
Sir: In response to your letter of the 8th inst., asking the co-operation of the Subsistence Department, I am directed to coöperate with the Association so far as to furnish subsistence to the sick and wounded soldiers.
"Very respectfully, your obedient servant,
" A. B. Eaton, *Lt.-Col. and A. C. G. S.*"

"New York, *April* 9, 1862.

"Dear Sir: I have received your favor of to-day, informing me that I had been elected a member of the New England Soldiers' Relief Association.

"I beg through you to thank the Association for the honor conferred upon me. Heartily sympathizing in the cause the Association has in charge, and myself engaged in a similar work, I shall not fail to do all in my power to promote that cause.

"Your obedient servant,
"George Bliss, jr.

Sec. N. E. S. Relief Association."

On motion of Mr. Paine, seconded by Col. Howe,

Dr. Eleazer Parmly, a native of Vermont, was unanimously elected a member of this Association.

Mr. Hawkins, from the Committee appointed for that purpose, reported:

That they had caused to be made the following books:

1st. Register.

2d. Index.

3d. Visitors' Book.

and now exhibit these books to the Association.

That this splendid set of books was made to order according to the express directions of the Committee, by the well-known firm of stationers, Messrs. Francis & Loutrel, and that those gentlemen, with great kindness and generosity, had sent in their bill receipted, accompanied by the following letter:

38

"New York, *April* 15, 1862.

"To Col. Frank E. Howe, *Gen. Supt. N. E. S. Relief Assoc.:*

"Dear Sir: Please do us the favor to present to the Association, with our best wishes, the accompanying books, which we have made for their use, and desire them to receive as a contribution toward the good work in which they are engaged.

"With respect, yours truly,
"Francis & Loutrel."

Whereupon,

On motion of Mr. Paine, seconded by Col. Howe, it was unanimously

Resolved, That the thanks of this Association be, and they are hereby, tendered to Messrs. Francis & Loutrel, for their very generous, acceptable, and appropriate gift of a splendid set of books.

Col. Howe desired to state to the meeting, that the very handsome and excellent carpet which covers this meeting room of the Association, was presented by Alexander T. Stewart, Esq., with his characteristic liberality.

Whereupon,

On motion of Judge Peabody, seconded by Maj. Pullen, it was

Resolved, That the thanks of this Association be, and they are hereby, tendered to Alexander T. Stewart, Esq., for the very handsome present of a carpet, which he has, with characteristic liberality, donated to the Association.

Judge Peabody presented the following letter from Dr. Edward W. Lambert, tendering his professional services:

"New York, *April* 14, 1862.
"Judge C. A. Peabody,

"Dear Sir: My professional services are at the disposal of the Committee in charge of the sick and wounded New England soldiers.

"Truly yours,
"E. W. Lambert, 330 Sixth Avenue."

Whereupon,

On motion of Mr. Fogg, seconded by Dr. Perkins, it was

Resolved, That the thanks of this Association be, and

39

they are hereby, tendered to Dr. Edward W. Lambert, for his humane and patriotic offer of professional services, and the same are gratefully accepted ; and that the Secretary be requested to notify Dr. Lambert of the action of this Association.

The Secretary, Dr. Maurice Perkins, stated to the meeting that he has continual calls from physicians heartily offering their services to this Association, and also from the two years' students in the College of Physicians and Surgeons, who are willing to spend day and night in rendering professional aid whenever it may be required.

On motion of Judge Peabody, seconded by Mr. Hawkins,

Mr. Hosea Ballou Perkins, a native of New Hampshire, was unanimously elected a member of this Association.

Mr. Hawkins made a statement in reference to the dimensions and capacity of the Association Building, as follows :

The house consists of four commodious floors, containing 16,000 square feet of space. The lower floor is divided into a committee-room and reception-room, the next two floors for dormitories, and the upper floor for kitchen, storage, and janitor's quarters.

Col. Howe stated that he would be able to procure the services of a nurse, assistant nurse, and janitor, whom he believed to be more than ordinarily qualified to fulfil the duties of an establishment like this one ; and that their entire services could be had at the rate of $600 per annum for all, and desired to know the pleasure of the Association.

Whereupon,

On motion of Judge Peabody, seconded by Mr. Paine, the whole matter was referred to Colonel Howe, Supt., with full authority to engage the persons referred to, at the rate of $600 per year, and to take whatever action in the matter may seem advisable to him.

Some remarks highly eulogistic of the taste, skill, and energy, displayed by Colonel Howe in getting the Association Building ready for occupancy, etc., were made by General Wetmore, upon whose motion, seconded by Judge Peabody, it was

Ordered, That the Secretary enter upon the minutes our unanimous and warm appreciation of the zeal, public spirit, taste, judgment, and devotion to duty so highly displayed by Colonel Howe, the superintendent, in fitting up and adapting to its uses this building, and of the very efficient manner in which he discharges the varied and onerous duties incident to his position as superintendent.

On motion of Colonel Howe, a recess was taken to inspect the building.

After a thorough inspection of the establishment, the gentlemen present returned to the committee-room, where they found prepared a handsome collation, which was presided over by Charles Gould, Esq., supported by Judge Bonney.

After the cloth was removed, the Chairman proposed the health of Colonel Howe, our Superintendent.

Which was responded to by Colonel Howe, who gave a history of the commencement, progress, and completion of the present undertaking.

Eloquent and appropriate speeches were also offered by the following gentlemen, who were called on to speak in the name of their respective States:

Rev. Dr. Hitchcock, for Maine.
Judge Bonney,   "   New Hampshire.
Dr. Parmly,   "   Vermont.
Rev. Dr. Osgood,   "   Massachusetts.
Mr. Hoppin,   "   Rhode Island.
Gen. Wetmore,   "   Connecticut.

Dr. Osgood also spoke in eulogy of New York, as did Judge Peabody.

Mr. Low and others followed.

Colonel Howe, in a very stirring and impressive speech, introduced Mr. R. G. Moulton, of New York, who was residing in Manchester, England, at the time of the attack upon Fort Sumter, and who was the prime mover and originator of the patriotic donation of a complete battery of Whitworth's rifled cannon by loyal American citizens in England and France, who took that method of testifying their devotion to their country's flag.

In the course of his remarks, Colonel Howe took occasion to state, that the Government had never yet made an acknowledgment of this patriotic gift, but on the contrary that Mr. Cameron, who was then Secretary of War, refused to have any thing to do with the guns, and it was with great difficulty that the War Department was finally induced to accept them ; and that they had never been put into service until the facts were brought to the knowledge of the President, Secretary Stanton, and General McClellan, the latter of whom immediately ordered them to be put into service in the attack upon Yorktown, and there they are now.

In conclusion, Colonel Howe hoped that this Association would hail the opportunity of being the first to recognize the patriotism, liberality, and devotion of Mr. Moulton and his associates abroad, and offered the following resolution :

Resolved, That the New England Soldiers' Relief Association, in behalf of the different States here represented, present their heartfelt thanks to R. G. Moulton, Esq., and his compatriots in England and France, for their generous donation to our common country, and for their efforts in its behalf on distant shores.

Judge Bonney, alluding in appropriate terms to the character of Mr. Moulton as a successful merchant at home and a patriotic American abroad, begged leave to second the resolution.

General Wetmore asked leave also to second the resolution. He was a member of the Union Defence Committee, and had had somewhat to do in respect to these guns, but until now had never heard the full history of the case.

That Committee was informed that some valuable guns

were lying upon the dock unprotected and exposed, and that one of them had been injured. The Committee took the guns in charge, and had them properly cared for.

The Committee also communicated with the U. S. military authorities. It was with great difficulty that they were induced to take these guns, but the Committee urged the matter, and they were sent to Governor's Island in the first place, subsequently removed to Washington, and now, as has been stated, are ranged in front of Yorktown defences.

The resolution was then unanimously adopted, with three times three for "our brothers abroad."

Mr. Moulton, in a modest and most eloquent speech, detailed the facts connected with the purchase and shipment of the guns, and the difficulties which they had to overcome before they could get them out of the country in the face of the Queen's proclamation. They finally arrived here in safety ; but Mr. Cameron had an idea that it must be some sort of a gun speculation, and of course was averse to being mixed up with any thing of that kind.

Disclaiming for himself and compatriots abroad, any merit for what they considered a sacred duty, Mr. Moulton concluded amidst loud applause.

On motion it was

Resolved, That Messrs. Howe, Bonney, and Wetmore be a committee to transmit the resolution just passed, to Mr. Moulton and our friends in England and France, who joined in the patriotic donation, and to place the matter rightly before the public.

Colonel Howe brought to the notice of the Association the kindness and attention of Colonel Almy to certain wounded soldiers who were not Connecticut men;

And referred to the assistance and coöperation of Mr. Hawkins in the work of the Association ;

And offered the following resolution, which was unanimously adopted :

Resolved, That the thanks of this Association are due to Colonel John H. Almy, for his kind attention to wounded soldiers, who, not belonging to the State of which he is agent, had no claim upon his official attention ; and to Dexter A. Hawkins, Esq., for his valuable coöperation with the Superintendent in the general work of the Association.

Adjourned to meet at the call of the Secretary.

MAURICE PERKINS, *Secretary.*

.

"NEW ENGLAND SOLDIERS' RELIEF ASSOCIATION."

SPECIAL MEETING OF THE ASSOCIATION.

New York, *Tuesday, April* 22, 1862.

The Association met this day pursuant to notice, at the Association Building, No. 194 Broadway.

Present, Messrs.

Andrews,	Bonney,	Bond,
Burns,	Gould,	Hawkins,
Hoppin,	Howe,	Knight,
Low,	McCurdy,	Paine,
Peabody,	Perkins,	Pullen,
	Wetmore.	

The Chairman and Vice-Chairman being absent, the meeting was called to order at half-past 4 o'clock p. m., by General Wetmore, on whose motion

John Paine, Esq., was called to the chair.

The minutes of the last preceding meeting were read and approved.

The Chairman stated the object for which the meeting had been called, which was to consider the propriety of taking certain measures for increasing the funds of the Association beyond the amount at first suggested.

Mr. Gould, the Vice-Chairman, having arrived, at the request of Mr. Paine, took the chair, and made further statements in reference to the object of the meeting.

Col. Howe, Superintendent, made a statement of the expenses of the Association thus far, which amounted to $1,290, and covered all the bills for arranging the building, including plumbing, gas fitting, carpenters' work, &c.

Col. Howe then verbally reported upon the general affairs of the Association since the last meeting, and an informal discussion was had in relation thereto.

Col. Howe then read the following letter :

"New York, *April* 7, 1862.

"Col. Frank E. Howe, No. 194 Broadway :

"Dear Sir : To the New England Association for the Relief of Sick and Disabled Soldiers returning from the battle-field, I offer most freely, whenever called upon, my services as surgeon.

"J. S. Kilbourne, M. D., No. 126 Franklin st."

And stated, that he had been requested by Dr. Alfred Underhill to offer his professional services to the Association.

And also that Mr. Charles A. Stetson, of the Astor House, had desired him to say, that the professional services of Dr. Swan were at the disposal of the Association, whenever required.

He had also received the following letter from Colonel Eaton :

"Office of Asst. Com. Gen. of Subsistence, }
"New York, *April* 16, 1862. }

"Col. Frank E. Howe, *Supt. of N. E. S. R. Assoc.*, 194 *Broadway, N. Y.*:

"Please, when you subsist sick and wounded soldiers on rations supplied by this Department, have the period during which they shall have been so subsisted endorsed on their papers, furlough, or discharge, thus :

"Subsisted at 194 Broadway, New York, from . .
to . . inclusive.
"For Subsistence Department, U. S. A.,
"By . . . .,"

and let the fact that such endorsement has been made, be noted on your book of records opposite each name.

"Very respectfully, your obedient servant,
"A. B. Eaton, *Lt.-Col. and A. C. G. S.*"

Col. Howe also stated that he had received from Dr. Vinton an account of his mission to Washington, but said that he should prefer to await a report from Dr. Vinton, personally, when he should be present with the Association.

Gen. Wetmore, on behalf of Dr. Gouverneur M. Smith, tendered his professional services to the Association.

The Secretary, Mr. Bond, presented and read the following letters:

"STATE OF VERMONT, EXECUTIVE DEPART- }
MENT, BRATTLEBORO, *April* 17, 1862. }

"WILLIAM BOND, Esq., *Sec. of the N. E. S. R. Assoc.*, 194 *Broadway, N. Y.:*

"DEAR SIR: I have the pleasure to acknowledge the receipt of a copy of the 'Minutes of the Organization and Proceedings of the New England Soldiers' Relief Association,' of New York, and your polite note therewith, informing me of my election as an Honorary Member of the Association. It is indeed an honor to be joined to such an Association, and I return you my hearty thanks for it.

"I have read the 'Minutes' with great interest and gratification. Nothing has occurred in our country, during the past eventful year, more honorable to humanity than the formation and efforts of this Association for the relief of sick and wounded soldiers on their return home from camp and battle-field. In our country's hour of peril and need, these brave men, with cheerful alacrity, *volunteered* to defend it ; and now, in their hour of suffering, your Association ministers to their relief.

"On behalf of the State of Vermont, I return thanks to your Association for their thoughtful, Christian kindness in making provision for the sick and wounded 'Green Mountain Boys' returning to their homes. Vermont will be happy to coöperate with your Association in the promotion of its humane and noble purposes.

"I am, with high regard, your obedient servant,

"FREDERICK HOLBROOK."

"STATE OF MAINE, EXECUTIVE DEPART- }
MENT, AUGUSTA, *April* 18, 1862. }

"WILLIAM BOND, Esq., *Sec., &c.:*

"DEAR SIR: I have your note informing me of my election as an Honorary Member of the New England Soldiers' Relief Association.

"I thank the Association for the honor it has done me, and I desire you to assure the thoughtful and humane gentlemen who compose it, that I will gladly coöperate with them so far as may be in my power, and that Maine will cheerfully contribute her quota of material aid to the noble work they have in hand.

"Very truly, your obedient servant,

"ISRAEL WASHBURN, jr."

The Secretary also presented a letter from Mr. R. H. McCurdy, acknowledging his election as a member of the Association.

Mr. McCurdy, who was present, stated his reasons for declining to serve on the Finance Committee, and repeated his request to be excused.

Whereupon, on motion of Mr. Paine, the declination of Mr. McCurdy was accepted; and

On motion of Mr. Paine, seconded by Mr. McCurdy, the question being put by Judge Peabody,

Charles Gould, Esq., was elected to fill the vacancy in the Finance Committee, caused by the resignation of Mr. McCurdy.

On motion, it was

Resolved, That the thanks of this Association be, and they are hereby, tendered to Doctors Kilbourne, Underhill, Swan, and Smith, respectively, for their humane and patriotic offers of professional aid, and the same are gratefully accepted; and that the Secretary be requested to notify those gentlemen severally of the action of this Association.

The Vice-Chairman then resumed the subject in reference to which this meeting had been called.

After an interchange of opinions, in which Messrs. Peabody, Wetmore, Gould, Paine, Low, Burns, and Howe, participated, it was decided to postpone the consideration of the subject until the next meeting.

On motion of General Wetmore, seconded by Colonel Howe, it was

Resolved, That the State Agent for Connecticut in this city, be invited to make use of such accommodations in this building as he may desire to avail himself of, for the purpose of transacting the business of his agency.

On motion, adjourned.

WILLIAM BOND, *Secretary.*

"NEW ENGLAND SOLDIERS' RELIEF ASSOCIATION."

SPECIAL MEETING OF THE ASSOCIATION.

NEW YORK, *April* 30, 1862.

PURSUANT to notice, the Association met at the Association Building, No. 194 Broadway, and was called to order at half-past seven o'clock P. M., by Mr. Gould, Vice-Chairman.

Present, Messrs.

HAWKINS,	BOND,	LOW,
HITCHCOCK,	PERKINS,	KNIGHT,
BONNEY,	BRIDGHAM,	HOPPIN,
PEABODY,	PARMLY,	ALMY,
PULLEN,	HOWE,	WETMORE,
PAINE,	WELLINGTON,	GOULD,
	OSGOOD.	

The minutes of the last meeting were read and approved.

Colonel Howe, the Superintendent, being called upon, reported verbally to the Association in relation to various matters of interest.

He stated that during the preceding two weeks fifty-two soldiers had been received and comfortably provided for at the Association Building, and that they belonged to the following States respectively, viz.:

Maine,	6	New York,	8
Vermont,	1	New Jersey,	8
Massachusetts,	18	Pennsylvania,	2
Rhode Island,	4	Missouri,	2
Connecticut,	3		—
			52

Also, that within the same time, one hundred and twenty-eight visitors have visited the Association Building and registered their names in the visitors' book, leaving unsolicited donations in money, to be used for the general purposes of the Association, amounting to a little over four hundred dollars, besides contributions of many useful articles.

He also stated that the Ladies' Committee for the preceding two weeks had, in addition to their incessant labors and untiring care at the Association Building, contributed largely in money and articles of necessity for the use of the Association, and in this connection submitted the following Report:

REPORT OF THE LADIES' COMMITTEE, FROM APRIL 25TH, 1862.

Articles Purchased for the N. E. S. Relief Association.

Stewart & Co.—Bill of Sundries,	.	$6 20
Haydock—Crockery,	. .	8 00
1 Bottle Sherry,	.	75
Dress for Soldier's Wife,		1 25
Stockings,	. . .	50
10 yards Towelling and 2 Rollers,	.	2 00
Tacks, Nails, Mucilage, and Ink,	.	36
Hagerty—Bill for Crockery,	.	6 00
J. S. Lane—Blue Cambric,		6 60
Windle—Refrigerator, &c.,	.	18 63
Casey—Tea Boiler,		6 00
Griffin & Titus—Crockery,		3 19
Evans—Crockery,	. . .	2 88
Windle—Rollers,	. .	1 80
Smith & Sons—Stoneware,		3 66
Provisions,	. . .	6 69
Dust-pan and Alcohol Feeder,	.	50
Windle—Sundry articles,	.	14 35
		$89 36

In payment of the above, cash contributed
as a donation to the N. E. S. R. Assoc. :

By Miss Woolsey,	$14 20	
" Mrs. G. W. Gray,	50 00	
" Mrs. S. Osgood.	25 16	
		$89 36

Donations.

1 box Clothing, from Seventh Presbyterian Church.
3 doz. Combs and Brushes, from Howard, Sanger & Co.
Labels, from Francis & Loutrel.
2 Jars Jelly, from Mrs. J. Wall.
Stranger, to Mrs. Sterling, $3.
1 Bottle Sherry Wine, from Mrs. Russell.
Cakes, Oranges, and Cocoa, from children of Mrs. Parkin.
Grape Jelly, Old Linen, from Mrs. Gould.
Box of Bandages and Lint, from Mrs. Gen. Tyler.
Drinking Cups and Spoons, from Norwalk Lock Co.
3 doz. Plated Spoons, from Hiram Young, 20 John st.
1 Eight-day Brass Clock, from George B. Owen, 25 John st.

Angelina Post, *in behalf of the Committee.*

April 29, 1862.

He also submitted to the meeting the following suggestions made by Mrs. Post, in writing, on behalf of the Ladies'
Auxiliary Committee:

"The ladies of the Second Committee, being entirely satisfied
of the necessity of having an experienced and judicious Matron to
take the general superintendence of the Soldiers' Home, are much
gratified that Mr. Howe has obtained a person with high testi-
monials, who seems in every way qualified to undertake the arduous
duties of this establishment.

"In their opinion, it will be necessary that she should have the
charge of all the supplies, the care of the house linen and clothing
of the establishment; to use her discretion in giving the latter to
such patients as require garments; to have charge of all the deli-
cacies that may be sent for the use of the sick; and to keep an account of all donations received, to report weekly; to make, *herself,* any kind of nourishment required for the invalids unable to
take the meals furnished for the convalescent; and to administer in
every way to the needs and comfort of the inmates of this establishment.

"She is also to see that order and cleanliness is everywhere
preserved throughout the premises; to see that the food generally
is properly prepared, and with proper liberality in regard to the
supplies, to avoid, as far as possible, any unnecessary waste.

"As far as the observation of the ladies in so short a time has resulted, they are of opinion that the women now employed, or who may hereafter be employed by the Association, should act under the instructions of the Matron. If, after a fair trial, they are found to be unequal to their duties, justice to the Matron will require their discharge.

"In regard to the washing, some arrangement with a laundry by the month would seem to be the best arrangement. The washing will be of the plainest description, requiring no starch, but the bedding should be returned thoroughly clean and well aired; the Matron to see that the returns are correct.

"In regard to the supplies of butcher's meat, an account with some butcher should be kept, whereby, in case of an emergency (the absence of Col. Howe or the gentlemen of the Committee) she could obtain what might be requisite, so as to have it prepared in due season. The men who can eat, require a good meal of fresh provisions, *not government rations*, which cannot be prepared in time for those who are to be forwarded immediately.

"These suggestions are respectfully submitted by

"MRS. POST,

"*In behalf of the Ladies of the Committee.*

"*April 29th, 1862.*"

And stated that, agreeing with the Ladies' Committee as to the importance of having a Matron in constant attendance at the Association Building, he had, with the advice and approval of the "Women's Auxiliary Committee," engaged Mrs. M. Squire to fill that position; and thereupon read several letters recommending Mrs. Squire, and endorsing her peculiar fitness and capacity for such a situation.

Colonel Howe then made a statement in relation to the arrival of one hundred and fifty wounded soldiers on the steamer Cossack and their passage through the city, specifying the attentions shown to them on behalf of this Association by Colonel Almy and himself, and expressing the decided conviction arrived at by the several State Agents that it is wrong and inexpedient to endeavor to hurry wounded soldiers through New York immediately on their arrival.

He also called to the attention of the Association the fact

that Col. Tompkins, A. Q. M. General, had appointed Mr. Thos. W. Johnson as an assistant to coöperate with the several State Agents in receiving and providing for the sick and wounded soldiers who shall arrive in this city; and, after expressing his pleasure at the appointment, and his gratification that a person possessing the ability and qualifications of Mr. Johnson had been designated for the position, he submitted the following correspondence connected with Mr. Johnson's appointment:

"Asst. Qr. M. General's Office,
"New York, *April 25th*, 1862.

"Sir: I hereby appoint you an assistant of this Department to look after and provide for the wants of the sick and wounded men who may arrive here from time to time, from the several army corps operating in the field.

"In the discharge of this duty, you are expected to use every possible exertion to provide in the most prompt and efficient manner for the wants, in the way of transportation or shelter, of all such persons of the above description as may arrive here and stand in need of assistance.

"You will confer with Col. Bliss, at No. 5 Walker street, Aide-decamp to Gov. Morgan, Col. F. E. Howe, No. 194 Broadway, Asst. Q. M. General of the State of Massachusetts and Agent for the State of Vermont, and Col. J. H. Almy, Asst. Q. M. General of the State of Connecticut, in relation to the duties with which you are charged, so far as relates to the men who belong to the respective States which they represent.

"It is expected that you will visit each vessel in the Government service which may arrive here with sick and wounded men on board belonging to the army, make a list of all such persons, designating those who may be able to travel by the ordinary modes of conveyance, and who wish to return to their homes, as of the first class, and such as may be unable to travel, and require medical treatment, as the second class, and state the respective places of destination of all those described as the first class.

"In all your duties you are expected and strictly enjoined to leave nothing undone which it may be in your power to do to alleviate the sufferings of those who may be so unfortunate as to require your attention and care.

"You are required to report at this office at least once a day, and as much oftener as the nature of your duties will admit, and to make weekly reports in writing of all your transactions during the week, and to keep a record of service in a book which will be furnished you for the purpose.

"I am, Sir, very respectfully, your ob't servant,

"D. D. TOMPKINS, *Asst. Qr. M. General.*

"MR. THOS. W. JOHNSON, *New York.*"

"ASST. QM.-GEN'LS OFFICE, }
"NEW YORK, *April 29th,* 1862. }

"COL. FRANK E. HOWE, *Asst. Qm.-Genl. State of Mass., &c. :*

"DEAR SIR: I herewith hand you a copy of instructions which I have received from the head of this Department, Col. D. D. Tompkins, Asst. Qm.-Gen'l. U. S., relative to the reception and care of the sick and wounded soldiers arriving at this point from the various departments of the army in the field, on the way to their respective homes.

"In carrying out these instructions, it becomes my duty, as it will be my pleasure, to confer and coöperate with the several State agencies and Relief Associations having in view the most ample provision for the reception, comfort, and kindly treatment of these returned sick and wounded 'Children of the Republic.'

"It is not the purpose of the agency established by the Government in this connection to subvert, but rather to coöperate in every practicable way with the patriotic Relief Associations of the city and the organizations of the several States represented here by local agencies, which were early prompted, and have been brought into existence by the highest considerations of humanity, and which have already accomplished so much good. But recognizing this as a legitimate duty of the Government, and fearing that *an entire miscellaneous effort* might fail in the full realization of the end which we all desire, this farther provision has been deemed advisable.

"The great number of invalid soldiers which the approaching sickly season must throw upon our hands, together with the unavoidable casualties of the terrible conflict now near at hand, will require the most untiring and hearty zeal and coöperation of all the means and agencies which have already or may hereafter be devised for the proper reception and care of the brave unfortunate men who may at any moment be precipitated upon us. Let no effort, therefore, be relaxed to make ample provision for any and every emergency.

"I would beg leave to suggest the propriety of hereafter detaining the returning invalid soldiers 'as they arrive in this city, long enough to properly cleanse them from the accumulation of filth unavoidable to a lengthy sea voyage, and to provide them with a change of clean underclothing, at least, which is so essential to their health and comfort, and that they may carry with them to their homes the evidence of the care and attention they received while passing through New York.

"Very respectfully, your obedient servant,

"THOMAS W. JOHNSON, *Asst. to Qr. M. Dept.*"

"NEW YORK, *April* 30, 1862.

"THOMAS W. JOHNSON, Esq., *Asst. to Quartermaster's Dept.*:

"DEAR SIR: We wish to acknowledge your favor of April 29th, accompanied by a copy of your instructions received from the head of the Quartermaster's Department located in this city.

"We are happy to know, that Government duly appreciates the importance of coöperating with the several States in their efforts to alleviate the sufferings and add to the comforts of those brave men who have so nobly fallen on the battle-field, and who are daily arriving here in a helpless and destitute condition.

"It will be our pleasure to confer with you in reference to the best modes of carrying out the objects proposed, and we shall be at all times happy to meet you and labor for a common end.

"Respectfully, yours,

"FRANK E. HOWE,

"J. H. ALMY."

After the foregoing correspondence had been read, Gen. Wetmore offered the following resolutions, which were unanimously adopted:

Resolved, That this Association appreciates and gratefully acknowledges the courtesy and high sense of duty and patriotic devotion shown by Col. Tompkins, Asst. Quartermaster-General, U. S. A., in the appointment of a special agent of that Department to unite with the executive officers of this Association, in assisting to forward to their homes, with comfort and despatch, sick and wounded soldiers who may arrive in this city.

Resolved, That a copy of the foregoing resolution be transmitted to the Secretary of War and to Col. Tompkins.

The following communication from Gov. Andrew was read and ordered to be recorded with the minutes:

"COMMONWEALTH OF MASSACHUSETTS, EXECUTIVE)
DEPARTMENT, BOSTON, *April* 26, 1862. }

" WILLIAM H. L. BARNES, Esq., *Cor. Sec. N. E. S. R. A., New York :*

" SIR: I have had the pleasure to receive a pamphlet copy of the minutes of the organization and proceedings of your Association, and also to receive information that it has conferred upon me the honor of an election to its membership.

"I pray you to convey to the Association my sincere thanks for allowing me the privilege of being united with its members, with ever so slight an opportunity of sharing in a work so humane, so useful, and so worthy. I am sure that in many Massachusetts homes, the kindness experienced by our soldiers in the city of New York will never be forgotten.

" I am, with sincere good wishes and much respect,

" Your obliged and obedient servant,

" JOHN A. ANDREW."

Attention was called by Mr. Paine to the fact that no formal recognition had been made by this Association, of the offer of professional services made by the New York Surgical Aid Association.

Whereupon,

The following resolution was offered by Mr. Gould, and unanimously adopted:

Resolved, That the thanks of this Association be, and they are hereby, tendered to the "New York Surgical Aid Association," for their humane and patriotic offer of professional services, and the same are gratefully accepted; and that the Secretary be requested to notify them of the action of this Association.

The subject of a Resident House Physician for the Association Building was discussed at some length, and was finally referred to Messrs. Howe and Almy, to make such arrangements as they may deem proper in relation to the matter.

Col. Almy, being called upon, made some interesting statements connected with the arrival of the last detachment of wounded New England soldiers. He also made particular mention of the thoughtful kindness of the ladies who compose the "Soldiers' Aid Society" of Stamford, Conn., who, on being informed that a number of wounded soldiers were in the cars and would pass through that place, were in waiting at the depot, on the arrival of the train, and carried into the cars refreshments of various descriptions, and gratuitously distributed them among the invalid soldiers.

He offered the following resolution in recognition of this tender care by the ladies of Stamford, which was unanimously adopted:

Resolved, That the grateful acknowledgments of this Association be tendered to the Ladies Soldiers' Aid Society of Stamford, represented by Mrs.Truman Smith, their President, for their kind and benevolent care extended to the New England wounded soldiers when on their way homeward, on Friday, the 25th inst.; and that the Secretary is requested to inform Mrs. Smith of the action of this Association.

The following communication was then presented and read:

"NEW YORK, *April* 30, 1862.

"DEAR SIR: Please offer my professional services to the New England Relief Association, to attend the sick and wounded New England heroes by day or night.

"Respectfully, yours,

"F. WILLIS FISHER, M. D.,

"237 West 14th st.

"WM. M. EVARTS, Esq., *Chairman N. E. R. Assoc.*"

Whereupon, on motion of Mr. Knight, it was

Resolved, That the thanks of this Association be, and they are hereby, tendered to Dr. Fisher for his humane and patriotic offer of professional services, and the same are

gratefully accepted; and that the Secretary be requested
to notify Dr. Fisher of the action of this Association.

A communication was read from Rev. Dr. Bellows, tendering, in behalf of Dr. R. P. Stevens, 244 Canal street, his
professional services to this Association.

Whereupon,

On motion of Judge Bonney, it was

Resolved, That the thanks of this Association be, and they
are hereby, tendered to Dr. Stevens for his humane and
patriotic offer of professional services, and the same are
gratefully accepted; and that the Secretary be requested
to notify Dr. Stevens of the action of this Association.

Judge Peabody, on behalf of Wm. B. Dinsmore, Esq.,
President of the Adams Express Company, offered to this
Association, for the purpose of conveying wounded soldiers
that may arrive in this city, the gratuitous use of any number, from one to twenty, of their express wagons, and
stated that they would with pleasure furnish horses, wagons,
and drivers for this benevolent purpose, at any hour of the
day or night that they should be called upon to do so.

Whereupon,

On motion of Judge Peabody, it was unanimously

Resolved, That the thanks of this Association be, and they
are hereby, tendered to the Adams Express Company, and
to William B. Dinsmore, Esq., President, for their liberal,
humane, and patriotic offer, which is gratefully accepted;
and the Secretary is requested to notify Mr. Dinsmore of
the action of this Association.

The following communication from the Board of Commissioners of Health was read to the meeting by Colonel
Howe :

"At a meeting of the Board of Commissioners of Health.

"MAYOR'S OFFICE, NEW YORK, *April* 22, A. D. 1862.

"Present,

"Hon. GEORGE OPDYKE, Mayor, presiding.

"   JOHN T. HENRY, Pres. of the Board of Aldermen.

"   CHARLES C. PINCKNEY, Pres. of the Bd. of Councilmen.

58

"Dr. Lewis Sayre, Resident Physician.

"Dr. Jehediah Miller, Health Commissioner.

"A communication was received from Col. Frank E. Howe, Military Agent for Massachusetts and Vermont, requesting special permit for transmission of dead bodies of soldiers through the city, without the delay incident to the production of testimony and obtaining of permits in each case.

"Whereupon it was,

"On motion of Dr. Sayre, Resident Physician,

"*Resolved,* That the City Inspector be directed to grant to Col. Howe, and other military agents, a general permit for the transmission from this city, without examination or other detention, of dead bodies of soldiers passing through the city in transition to their place of burial elsewhere; and that Col. Howe and the other agents acting upon such permits, report their action thereunder to the City Inspector as often as he may require.

"Extract from the Minutes.

"Wm. H. Armstrong, *Clerk.*"

Whereupon,

On motion of Col. Howe, it was,

Resolved, That the thanks of this Association be, and they are hereby, tendered to the Board of Commissioners of Health, for their considerate and humane action in directing the City Inspector to grant to the several State Agents special facilities for the transmission from this city of dead bodies of soldiers passing through the city to their place of burial elsewhere.

The Secretary announced the following Visiting Committees, in addition to those previously designated :

For the Week ending May 22d.

Gen. Prosper M. Wetmore,   Dr. Maurice Perkins,
Dr. Eleazar Parmly,   Hon. Rufus F. Andrews.

For the Week ending May 29th.,

Rev. Dr. Hitchcock,   Samuel W. Bridgham, Esq.,
John Paine, Esq.,   William J. Hoppin, Esq.

For the Week ending June 5th.

Rev. Dr. Osgood,　　　　Hon. Charles A. Peabody,
Maj. J. A. Pullen,　　　　Jeremiah Burns, Esq.

For the Week ending June 12th.

Nehemiah Knight, Esq.,　　Charles Gould, Esq.,
R. H. McCurdy, Esq.,　　　Hon. B. W. Bonney.

For the Week ending June 19th.

Rev. Dr. Vinton,　　　　F. E. Wellington, Esq.,
Samuel E. Low, Esq.,　　William H. Fogg, Esq.

Also, that the weekly Visiting Committees of the Women's Auxiliary Association, for the same period, were as follows:

For the Week ending May 22d.

Mrs. R. R. Booth.　　　Mrs. George Brown,
Mrs. Hilliard,　　　　Mrs. Henry V. Poor,
Mrs. G. Kissell.　　　Miss Post.

For the Week ending May 29th.

Mrs. John Paine,　　　Mrs. H. B. Smith.
Miss Jane S. Woolsey,　Mrs. Dr. Gurdon Buck,
Mrs. R. D. Hitchcock,　Mrs. Charles Perkins.

For the Week ending June 5th.

Mrs. Samuel Osgood,　　Mrs. A. Brookes,
Mrs. J. Nelson Tappan,　Mrs. A. C. Richards,
Mrs. J. W. Post,　　　Mrs. W. G. Sterling.

For the Week ending June 12th.

Mrs. Charles Gould,　　Mrs. E. B. Merrill,
Mrs. Andrew Wesson,　　Mrs. M. O. Roberts,
Miss Hale,　　　　　Miss Annie Potts.

For the Week ending June 19th.

Mrs. FRANK E. HOWE,   Mrs. E. V. HAUGHWOUT,
Mrs. F. E. WELLINGTON,   Mrs. E. W. STOUGHTON,
Mrs. H. W. HUBBELL,   Mrs. FREDERICK SWAN.

On motion,

Adjourned, to meet on Wednesday, May 14th, at 194 Broadway, at 7½ o'clock P. M.

WILLIAM BOND, *Secretary.*

TREASURER'S REPORT.

The Treasurer of the New England Soldiers' Relief Association acknowledges the receipt of contributions in money, for the uses of the Association, from the following persons respectively, viz. :

Hoyt, Sprague & Co.,	$200	William M. Evarts,	$50
Samuel Wetmore,	200	Peter Richards, Jr.,	50
Elias Howe, Jr.,	100	Hoyt Brothers,	50
A. A. Low & Brothers,	100	The Misses Woolsey,	50
Weston & Gray,	100	E. D. Morgan & Co.,	50
William H. Fogg,	100	R. P. Buck,	50
Nehemiah Knight,	100	Snow & Burgess,	50
Edwin Hoyt,	100	David Oliphant,	50
Duncan, Sherman & Co.,	100	Read, Gardner & Co.,	50
J. A. Pullen,	100	Amos R. Eno,	50
Jonathan Sturgis,	100	Low, Harriman & Co.,	50
Moses H. Grinnell,	100	Thomas Dunham & Co.,	50
Charles Mixter,	100	Daniel G. Bacon,	50
John Paine,	100	Jacob Harsen,	50
Nathl. L. & George Griswold,	100	James Howe,	25
E. H. Stoughton,	100	H. P. Sturgis & Co.,	25
First Cong. Church, Fairfield,		Archer & Bull,	25
Conn.,	60	Howland & Frothingham,	25
Beebe & Brother,	50	W. A. & A. M. White,	25
Benj. B. Sherman,	50	Bowerman Brothers,	25
John Caswell & Co.,	50	A. & E. Robbins,	25
Anthony & Hall,	50	Frothingham & Baylis,	25
Ward & Co.,	50	R. Sands Tucker,	25
Charles H. Marshall,	50	Beebe, Montgomery & Co.,	25
Samuel L. M. Barlow,	50	Dexter A. Hawkins,	25
C. Maverick Parker,	50	E. Parmly,	25
Spofford & Tileston,	50	Charles P. Kirkland,	25
William Curtis Noyes,	50	William G. Lambert,	25

Augustus Cleveland,	. . . $25	Wm. A. Walker & Co.,	. . . $20
C. B. Tatham,	 25	H. B. Watson,	 15
Samuel E. Low,	 25	A. Healy,	 11
Edwin Bartlett,	 25	Francis Skiddy,	 10
Bullard & Co.,	 25	Samuel Osgood,	 10
Young, Schultze & Co.,	. . 25	R. D. Hitchcock,	 10
Isaac H. Bailey,	 25	Francis Hathaway,	. . . 10
Rees & Hoyt,	 25	Gillespie & Studwell,	. . . 10
Jeremiah Burns,	 25	W. H. Gilman,	 10
A Friend,	 25	W. M. Rogers & Co.,	. . . 10
Wm. H. Gilson,	 25	Mr. H. H., of Canada,	. . 10
Wetmore, Cryder & Co.,	. . 25	Ethelbert S. Mills,	. . . 10
Earle & Co.,	 25	W. W. Chapin,	 10
G. R.,	 25	M. W. Terrill,	 10
Wallace & Wickes,	. . . 25	Mr. Sweet,	 5
Cyrus W. Field,	 25	A. B. Morgan,	 5
O. H. Gordon & Co.,	. . . 25	George H. Francis,	 5
Joseph A. Alsop,	 25	Moses Allen,	 5
Walsh, Carver & Chase,	. . 25	Mrs. Mary Andrews,	. . . 5
Charles E. Hill & Co.,	. . 25	Cash,	 5
Cary & Co.,	 25	"	 5
Homer H. Stuart,	. . . 25	"	 5
Abner Beers,	 25	"	 5
Mrs. F. G. Swan,	 25	Mrs. Adriance,	 1
Charles Jarvis,	 20		
Edward T. Young,	 20		$4,272
George A. Talbot,	 20		

SAMUEL E. Low, Treasurer,
No. 31 Burling Slip.

Donations of Articles for the use of the Association, received by the Visiting Committees or Superintendent, at No. 194 Broadway.

Contributions in money received by the Treasurer, Mr. Samuel E. Low, No. 31 Burling Slip.